ed
A Cup of Mint Tea

Short Stories to Warm the Heart
Volume 1

BY IMAN ABDALLAH AL-QAISI

Illustrator: Nadia Yousef
Layout and Graphics: Zaid Al-Dabbagh
www.pandauxstudio.com
Translators: Afraa Jasim
Ranya Badawi
Hanan Abu Salah
Copy Editors: Fatma Almaery
Dima Almeniawi
Jackie Othman

DEDICATION

For those lost in the waves of life, searching for glimpses of hope and guidance ... For those walking in the path towards Allah (SWT), desperate for a rescue rope ... For those overwhelmed by the fast pace of life, and searching for a soothing sip of tea ...

For my dad, for letting me find my passion, supporting me in the hardest time, helping me be who I am today.

For my husband, for being the supportive husband he is, for his encouraging words.

For my family and friends who have supported and been there for me during every step and hardship through my journey.

For all those who helped make this book what it is, without you, this book would have never seen the light ...

Before all, to the Almighty Allah (SWT), for His help, guidance and blessing ... Whatever is good in this book is from Him, whatever is false is from myself and Satan.

To them, I dedicate this book ...

CONTENTS

The Virtue of Reading Quran Everyday - The Coal Basket 2
Live by the Verses of the Quran 6
Quran is Light 12
Quran for Healing (Ruqya) 16
Martyrdom of 'Umar Ibn Al-Khattab 22
The Importance of Perfecting Prayer 26
The Importance of Friday Prayer 32
Reverence in Prayer 38
The Importance of Fajr Prayer 42
The Importance of Praying with a Group 48
Midnight Prayers 54
Honesty is Your Protector 60
Being Truthful With the Prophet (PBUH) 66
Price of Honesty 74
Abu Hanifa and the Atheist 80

"If the hearts are pure, they will never satisfy their hunger for the Book of Allah."

Uthman Ibn Affan
May Allah be pleased with him

1
The Virtue of Reading Quran Everyday - The Coal Basket

An elderly man lived on a farm in the mountains of eastern Kentucky with his young grandson. Every morning the grandfather woke up early, and sat at the kitchen table reading from the Quran. His grandson wanted to be just like him and tried to imitate him every way he could.

One day the grandson asked, "Grandpa, I try to read the Quran just like you but I don't understand it, and what I do understand I forget as soon as I close the book. What good is reading the Quran?"

The grandfather quietly turned from putting coal in the stove and replied, "Take this coal basket down to the river and bring me back a basket of water." The boy did as he was told, but all the water leaked out before he got back to the house. The grandfather laughed and said, "You'll have to move a little faster next time," and sent him back to the river with the basket to try again.

This time the boy ran faster, but again the basket was empty before he returned home. Out of breath, he told his grandfather that it was impossible to carry water in a basket, and he went to get a bucket instead. The old man said, "I don't want a bucket of water, I want a basket of water. You're not trying hard enough," and he went out the door to watch his grandson try again.

At this point the boy knew it was impossible. However, he wanted to show his grandfather that even if he ran as fast as he could the water would leak out before he could return to the house. The boy dipped the basket into the river again and ran even faster, but when he reached his grandfather the basket was empty again. Out of breath, he said, "See Grandpa, it's useless!"

"So you think it is useless?" The old man said, "Look at the basket."

The boy looked at the basket and for the first time realized that the basket was different. It had been transformed from a dirty, old coal basket to a bright, clean basket inside and out. "Son, that's what happens when you read the Quran. You might not understand or remember everything, but when you read it you will be changed inside and out. That is the work of Allah in our lives."

Source: Multaqa Shadharaat al-Arab, from Qism Al-Dawa Al-Islami wal-Tansir

Lessons Learned:

1. **Respect Our Children**
   We should respect our children and not belittle them when they don't understand a matter. The grandfather didn't make fun of his grandson for not understanding the Quran. Rather, he was kind and taught him a great lesson.
2. **No Wrong Questions, Only Wrong Answers**
   A very important principle that should be taught to our children is that there are no wrong questions but often there are many wrong answers. A question can lead a person to understand great matters if answered correctly. We should encourage children to ask questions for two good reasons:
   a. To build stronger personalities.
   b. To expand their knowledge and open their minds.
3. **Active Learning**
   Visual connection is really important in delivering a concept. In this story we understand how the Quran purifies our hearts even if we do not understand the meaning of the book. We understand this by seeing that the basket became clean even though the boy had no intention in doing so, nor did he use anything meant to clean it. The Quran removes sickness and impurities from our hearts, even if we don't understand it. One can only imagine what it could do when one does understand the meaning!
4. **Various ways to Preach**
   There are various ways to deliver the message of Islam. Many people believe that the only way is through advice and lectures. The truth is that actions speak louder than words. In our practical example, the grandfather was able to make his point clear with an errand. He could have lectured his grandson for hours but would not have been able to deliver his message with such power.

"If you desire true knowledge, then dive into the Quran; for it has the knowledge of the past and of the future."

Abdallah Ibn Masud
May Allah be pleased with him

2
Live by the Verses of the Quran

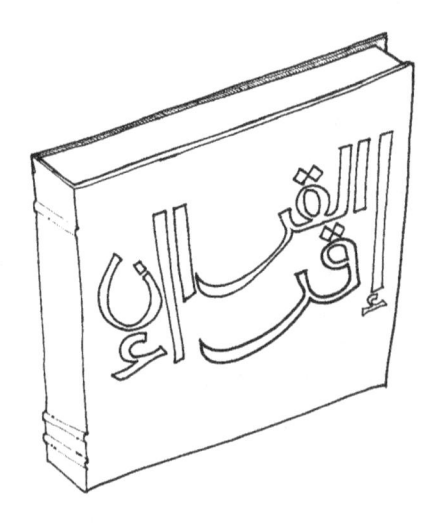

One day a young boy named Saeed Bin Al-Musayyib came to the great companion Zaid Ibn Thabit (The Prophet's (PBUH) translator and Quran transcript writer). He was only 12 years old at that time and he asked him "Give me advice that will guide me to live by in my life, to enter Paradise, and to guarantee my happiness in this life."

Zaid answered, "Live by these two verses: "And what is the life of this world except the enjoyment of delusion." [Al-i-Imran:185] and "And whoever honors the symbols of Allah - indeed, it is from the piety of hearts." [Al-Hajj:32]". He concluded by saying, "Recite the Quran until you find a verse that resonates and touches your heart, and live by that verse."

From that day on, Saeed began reciting the Quran, contemplating each verse and living by it. The first verse that affected him and in which he lived by was: "[Such niches are] in mosques which Allah has ordered to be raised and that His name be mentioned therein" [An-Nur:36]. From that day, he vowed to only pray in the masjid and never leave the front row during prayer. He never missed the opening "takbeer" in those 40 years and never prayed behind anyone but the Imam.

After a while, he was moved by another verse: "Righteousness is not that you turn your faces toward the east or the west, but [true] righteousness is [in] one who believes in Allah, the Last Day, the angels, the Book, and the Prophets (PBUH) and gives wealth, in spite of love for it, to relatives, orphans, the needy, the traveler, those who ask [for help], and for freeing slaves; [and who] establishes prayer and gives zakah; [those who] fulfill their promise when they promise; and [those who] are patient in poverty and hardship and during battle. Those are the ones who have been true, and it is those who are the righteous." [Al-Baqara:177]. He lived by this verse by determining never to go through a week without giving charity to the six groups mentioned in the verse.

Then he was touched by a third verse which was: "Only those fear Allah, from among His servants, who have knowledge" [Fatir:28]. He determined to learn Islamic knowledge and became a master scholar and the most knowledgeable in the matters of halal and haram and a scholar of the Prophet's (PBUH) companions. He was also a scholar of Hadith. Saeed Bin Al-Musayyib had acquired all this knowledge because he lived by the Quran.

Source: Saeed Bin Al-Musayyib, from the series "Ma' al-Tabi'een" by Dr. Amr Khaled, among other sources including Ibn Kathir, Ibn Hazm, Ibn Taymiyyah, and the book Siyar Ahwal al-Nubala'

Lessons Learned:

1. **Good Role Models and Their Impact on Young People**
   We note here that the young man Saeed, looked upon the companion as a good role model and sought his advice. This reflects Saeed's intelligence and cleverness. Rarely do we see young people seeking wisdom from good role models and rarely do we find role-models whose actions reflect their words.
2. **Wisdom in Giving Advice**
   Notice how Zaid directly responded to Saeed's request by telling Saeed to concentrate on the two verses and not the whole Quran. Zaid's wisdom was further revealed when he told Saeed to search for verses that resonate in his heart and touch him deeply.
3. **Asking Simple Questions**
   Saeed focused on three points in his request, which were: benefit and happiness in this life, and benefit in the afterlife. Being specific yet concise is essential in getting clear answers.
4. **Offering Advice No Matter How Small**
   Life with its beauty will eventually perish and we will be judged by Allah (SWT) for our deeds. Allah (SWT) will praise all acts of worship no matter how small or trivial they may seem.
5. **Living by the Quran**
   One of the first step to living the Quran is to pray in the masjid. Saeed learned that prayer should be in the masjid; prayer is the relationship between a Muslim and Allah (SWT). Performing prayer in the masjid promotes the relationship between a Muslim and other Muslims and it also tests one's patience and tolerance of others while praying. This verse teaches spiritual, social and physical discipline.
6. **Economic Responsibility**
   The second verse (Giving charity) taught Saeed about

the diverse groups to whom a Muslim should give. It also taught him that giving is not limited only to giving money, but it includes visiting others and smiling in others' faces, so he visited widows, orphans, and the needy. He would attend to their affairs and console them. He understood the verse for its true meaning and reflected the meaning of the verse with his actions.

7. **Education is the Key to Accomplishment**
   This is reflected by the third verse; Saeed delved into Islamic knowledge in order to deliver this knowledge with a clear vision and in a precise manner.

8. **Responding to Advice and Working by it**
   Many of us hear advice. Some decide to shun their ears to this advice and are at great loss. However, those who listen but do not act upon the advice are among the ignorant. But those who listen and act upon the advice are among the winners.

"And thus We have revealed to you an inspiration of Our command. You did not know what is the Book or [what is] faith, but We have made it a light by which We guide whom We will of Our servants. And indeed, [O Muhammad], you guide to a straight path"

[Ash-Shura:52]

3
Quran is Light

Usaid Bin Hudair a companion of the Prophet (PBUH), was known for his beautiful recitation of the Quran. One starry night, he went out for a stroll with his son Yahya to check on his horse. The horse was tied to a palm tree in their backyard.

The sky was bright, the stars were shinning, and the breeze was cool and calm. It was such a peaceful night. Soon enough his son Yahya, who was a young boy at the time, fell asleep near the horse under the palm tree.

Usaid thought to himself, "How delightful would it be to recite the Quran on such a beautiful night?" Usaid started to recite gracefully with his melodious voice: "In the name of Allah, Most Gracious, Most Merciful". "Alif, Lam, Meem. This is the Book about which there is no doubt, a guidance for those conscious of Allah" [Al-Baqara:1-2]. The horse suddenly became rowdy with excitement. Usaid did not want the horse to disturb his son, so he stopped reciting. The horse returned to being quiet, and so he resumed his recitation of the Quran: "Who believe in the unseen, establish prayer, and spend out of what We have provided for them" [Al-Baqara:3]. Again his horse began to move wildly about, neighing and kicking. Usaid paused for a second time, this time his mind was preoccupied with the safety of his son.

The horse calmed down, and Usaid resumed his recitation of the Quran: "Those are upon [right] guidance from their Lord, and it is those who are the successful." [Al-Baqara:5]. The third time, his horse moved wildly about. This time around, Usaid looked above him and saw a cloud, in fact, the most beautiful cloud he had ever seen! It was stunning; it looked as if it was illuminated with hundreds of lanterns. Usaid remained silent for the rest of the night, and watched as the cloud ascended up towards the heavens.

The next morning, Usaid ran to the Messenger of Allah to tell him all about what happened the night before. The Prophet (PBUH) said: "Recite, O Aba Yahya, those were the angels ... They descended from heaven to listen to your beautiful voice. And had you continued reciting through dawn, people would have been able to see them." (Narrated By Imam Bukhari)

Source: Usaid Bin Hudair from Rijal Hawl al-Rasul, page 286-287, by Khalid Mohammad Khalid

Lessons Learned:

The Importance of Family
People around the Prophet (PBUH) held on to the responsibility of their children. Usaid, wanted to spend some quality time with his son, he did not go out to enjoy his time alone. Spending time with your son doing something you both love is a great teaching opportunity. Remember parents are role models for their kids. Our children learn from our actions. Prophet Muhammad (PBUH) has encouraged us to teach our children horsemanship, to grow up fit and courageous.

1. **The Value of Time**
   Usaid did not waste any time. As soon as his son fell asleep he made good use of his time and began reciting Quran
2. **The Love of Quran and Learning How to Recite it to the Best of our Ability**
   The Prophet's (PBUH) companions knew the importance of the Quran, they memorized it and enjoyed reading it. Reciting Quran was not an obligation; it was joyful and rewarding to them.
3. **Quran is Light**
   The angels were so delighted to listen to Usaid as he was reciting, they didn't even try to hide. Perhaps, then, we should all watch what we are listening to ...
4. **Seeking Good Companions**
   We notice that the angels accompanied Usaid as long as he recited the Quran. Wouldn't we love to have angels for company? Would we ever be harmed by Satan?

"And We send down of the Qur'an that which is healing and mercy for the believers, but it does not increase the wrongdoers except in loss."

[Al-Isra:82]

4
Quran for Healing (Ruqya)

A group of the Prophet's (PBUH) companions set off on a journey. They had stopped at one of the villages in which the people of the book lived. The villagers welcomed them but refused to serve the companions food or even anything to drink, and in fact they did not offer them anything at all.

A while later, the leader of the village was bitten by a venomous creature. Everyone in the village attempted to cure the leader with no avail. The people suggested that someone ask the companions if they knew of a cure. A group of villagers then approached the companions and asked for their help. One companion said that he knew of a cure called (Ruqya), but since the villagers were not hospitable, he would not approach the leader unless they offered him something in return. The villagers said that they would give him a herd of sheep if he was able to heal the leader.

The companion approached the wounded leader and recited: "Al-Fatiha", "Al-Ikhlas", "Al-Falaq" and "Al-Nas". In no time, the leader arose as if nothing had happened to him. The villagers then offered the herd of sheep to the companions in return for the favor.

The companions were waiting for the herd of sheep to be divided amongst them, but the companion who had healed the leader declared that he would not divide the herd before he asked the Prophet (PBUH) about how it should be fairly divided and if what they had done was righteous. They approached the Prophet (PBUH) and narrated what had happened. The Prophet (PBUH) then asked them how they knew how to cure the injured leader. They replied by telling him (The Prophet (PBUH)) that they had learned it from him. The Prophet (PBUH) confirmed that what they had done was virtuous and that they must divide the herd of sheep among themselves including the Prophet (PBUH) in their division.

Source: Dalil al-Sa'ileen, pg 509, by Anas Ismail Abu Dawud

Lessons Learned:

1. **Hospitality and its Influence on People**
   A person must always be generous with his guests. Offering food and something to drink imposes love and mercy between both sides. When one mistreats a guest by not being hospitable, the guest will feel belittled and disregarded. Note that a person should not squander or waste with undue excess but should offer whatever he may have at home like a cup of coffee, a snack, or even a word of kindness.
2. **Value and Compensation**
   We notice that the Muslims asked for compensation in return for healing the leader because they wanted to show their value after the villagers had belittled them by not being hospitable. If they had been hospitable, the companions would not have asked for the compensation. This is why it is said: "Islam teaches us how to treat one another."
3. **Settling on an Agreement Before Initiating Any Act**
   In the story, the agreement was a herd of sheep given to the companions in exchange for healing the leader. This teaches us to declare what we expect before initiating an agreement, and if possible, to write agreements down so that neither party may defy the agreement causing harm to the other party.
4. **Healing with the Quran (Ruqya)**
   Scholars have confirmed that the Quran has an incredible power of healing, especially diseases linked to psychological and emotional problems. Ruqya alleviates all pains in addition to bestowing tranquility into the hearts of people. It also elevates the sick spiritually and psychologically. The Quran can be used to heal pain affecting any part of the body by rubbing that part and reading verses from the Quran. With Allah's will, that part will be cured, and at minimum the Ruqya will ease the pain.
5. **Consultation and Seeking Sustenance in Accordance to**

Islamic Law (Halal)
We note that the healer did not divide or take anything from the herd of sheep until he consulted the Prophet (PBUH) and confirmed that what he had done was in accordance with the laws of Islam. Here we learn that Muslims must fear Allah when initiating any act in order to avoid the haram of obtaining sustenance or money using methods not complying with Islamic Law. Allah (SWT) will not condone any money or sustenance obtained in the non-halal way.

Division and Justice
The reader may ask why the Prophet (PBUH) asked to receive his part. The Prophet (PBUH) had taught them the Ruqya and if it was not for him, they would not have known it. Whatever the Prophet (PBUH) received was always dispersed to the needy or used for the cause of Islam or the Muslims. As for the other companions, they had offered support and the companion's strength was multiplied by the number of companions accompanying him. If they had not been with the companion, the villagers would not have offered this large gratuity and would probably have offered him far less.

"Prayer: it multiplies your sustenance, protects your health, pushes away impurities, repels evil, strengthens the heart, enlightens the face, livens the soul, keeps laziness away, energizes the limbs, prolongs your strength, expands your chest, nourishes the soul, illuminates the heart, protects blessings, repels curses, attracts blessings, distances you from the devil."

Ibn Qayyim al-Jawziyya
May Allah have mercy on him

5
Martyrdom of 'Umar Ibn Al-Khattab

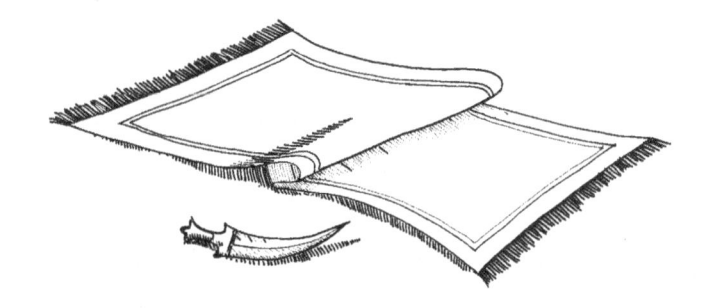

'Umar Ibn Al-Khattab (May Allah be pleased with him) was the second righteous caliph, and one of the ten companions promised paradise during their lifetimes.

Abu Lu'Lu' was a Zoroastrian (Fire-worshiper) who lived in Medina. At the time, Medina was the capital of the Islamic state. Abu Lu'Lu' had a plan. He poisoned a dagger and planned to attack 'Umar. Part of the caliph's job was also to be an Imam and lead Muslims in prayers so Abu Lu'Lu' snuck into the masjid and stabbed 'Umar with his dagger.

Abu Lu'Lu' stabbed 'Umar three times as he was leading the prayer of Fajr salah with the poisonous dagger and 'Umar tried to complete leading the Muslims in prayer, but his legs underneath him could no longer support him, because he had bled profusely. 'Umar, unable to continue leading the Muslims in prayer, took the hand of Abdulrahman ibn 'Awf and moved him forward so he could lead the remainder of the prayer.

The Muslims continued to pray, for those who were praying in the front rows behind 'Umar saw what happened, but those in the back of the masjid were unaware of what happened as they focused on their worship.

'Umar was carried to his home on the shoulders of some of the Muslims, where they tried to cure and treat him. 'Umar remained unconscious for a long time, but when he regained consciousness, he said, "Did the Muslims complete the morning prayer?" "Yes, we prayed, oh Amir al-Mumineen" they replied.

'Umar then asked, "Who stabbed me?" and they replied "Abu Lu'Lu' the Magian." 'Umar fell into sujud out of thankfulness, and said "All praise be to Allah, who caused my injury to be at the hands of a nonbeliever, who never prostrated to God a single prostration so that he might hold it as evidence against me in front of Allah on the Day of Judgement."

Source: Qissat Istish-had 'Umar Ibn Al-Khattab from, Dalil al-Sa'ileen, page 405, by Anas Ismail Abu Dawud

Lessons Learned:

1. **The Importance of Fajr Prayer**
   The companions of the Prophet (PBUH) hardly missed fajr prayer in congregation or any congregational prayer for that matter. The companions arranged their lives and activities around prayer times. This is what led Muslim scientists eventually to invent mechanical clocks! It is mentioned that one day Saed Ibn Al-Musayeb, a follower of the companions complained about his eyes. It was suggested to visit a park on the outskirts of Medina called Al-Aqeek to relax his eyes. Saed replied, "I can't go, because if I do, I will miss 'Isha and Fajr congregation prayers at the Masjid."
2. **Commitment to Prayer**
   When praying, you are standing in front of God, and nothing else on this earth matters. The Caliph was fatally injured, yet everyone who saw it kept calm; even 'Umar's greatest concern was for the Muslims to finish their prayer. Abdurrahman bin 'Awf finished the prayer and people in the back rows did not even know what had just happened.
3. **Muslims are Brothers to One Another**
   When finished praying, the companions rushed to check upon 'Umar (May Allah be pleased with them all). They wanted to stay close by him and help get him through this tough incident.
4. **Loving One Another For the Sake of Allah**
   'Umar thanked God that it was not a Muslim brother who had shed his blood because he did not want to be the cause of a Muslim brother receiving punishment from God.

Eagerness to Teach Up Until One's Final Moments
   The eagerness of 'Umar to revive and teach Prophet Muhammad's (PBUH) doctrine until his last moments. When 'Umar prostrated to thank God, he was trying to teach his fellow Muslims the Prophet's (PBUH) teachings on how to thank God.

"Prayer is a measurement, whoever remains loyal to it, will receive a greater reward. Whoever shortchanges it, for you have knowledge of what Allah the Almighty said about people who shortchange."

Salman Alfarsy
May Allah be pleased with him

— 6 —
The Importance of Perfecting Prayer

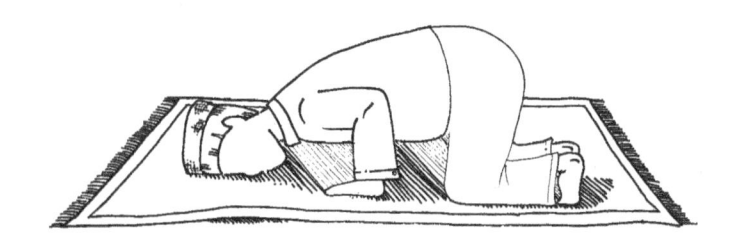

One day, Prophet Muhammad (PBUH) entered the mosque and a man came in and prayed. Then he came and greeted the Prophet (PBUH) by saying, "Assalamu Alaikum." The Prophet (PBUH) returned the greeting and said, "Go back and pray, for you have not prayed."

So he went back in a mannerly way, and prayed as he had prayed the first time. Then he returned and greeted the Prophet (PBUH) and the Prophet (PBUH) said, "Go back and pray for you have not prayed."

The man went again without discussing the matter with the Prophet (PBUH) and prayed. This happened three times and the fourth time the man wanted to know what he was doing wrong. He said, "By the One who sent you with the truth I cannot do any better; teach me."

The Prophet (PBUH) said, "When you stand to pray say takbir (Allahu Akbar). After that, recite whatever you can of Quran and then bow until you are at ease in bowing. Then stand up until you are standing straight and then prostrate until you are at ease in prostration. Then sit up until you are at ease in sitting. Do that throughout the whole prayer." The man then prayed in the manner the Prophet (PBUH) taught him.

Source: Hadith narrated by Al-Bukhari and Muslim

Lessons Learned:

1. **Returning Salam (Greeting) is an Obligation on Muslims**
   Although the Prophet (PBUH) was irritated from the man's fallible prayer, he returned the man's greeting for two reasons. The first reason was that returning a Muslims greeting is mandatory and the second reason was to assure him that the Prophet (PBUH) loved him and wanted what was best for him.
2. **Avoiding Retaliation or Argumentation**
   Note how the man went and prayed when the Prophet (PBUH) told him to repeat the prayer three times. He did not tell the Prophet (PBUH) to look at the way other people pray or point out their mistakes. He did not say that the Prophet (PBUH) was wrongfully accusing him of not praying correctly. On the contrary, the man listened and obeyed and did not seek retaliation because he felt that he was at fault. He did not argue either since he knew he would lose good deeds in what he does.
3. **Patience and Persistence**
   We notice that the man repeated his prayer 3 times before questioning the Prophet (PBUH) or asking him why he was telling him to repeat the prayer. This teaches us that when we want to teach someone a lesson, we must not rush in correcting mistakes and we must wait until the person at fault attempts to correct the mistake. Also, as learners, we must not ask about every detail, no matter how big or small, to know the purpose of the task.
4. **Tranquility and Prayer Acceptance**
   Tranquility in prayer is an important pillar for prayer acceptance; without it we will not be rewarded for our prayer. We must have tranquility and the presence of our hearts with Allah (SWT) as the essence of our prayer.
5. **Love of Knowledge and Promptness in Execution**
   Despite being told to repeat the prayer three times, the man

did not look at it negatively. On the other hand, he looked at the positive aspect of the request and asked the Prophet (PBUH) to teach him how to correct his mistake. Then he executed what he had learned and perfected his prayer.

6. **Listening and Obeying**
   The companions ensured that they listened and obeyed. If this occurred during our present time, one can only imagine when telling a person that he is not perfecting his prayer, that person would answer you with "Allah (SWT) will forgive me and He is the Merciful, and I will just be careful the next time I pray." That person might also initiate a fight or a harsh discussion. The companions always considered obedience and compliance as a law or a pillar that must never be forgotten.

7. **Perfection in All We Do and Being Rewarded**
   Many good deeds are not accepted because they were not done correctly. We must learn how to obey and learn the correct way to perform good deeds. We must choose good seeds to find the fruits in Heaven. On the Day of Judgment, we do not want to regret any prayer we did not pray correctly or any recitation from the Quran that was not done correctly because it would be as if we had done nothing in this life, may Allah (SWT) forbid.

"I swear that Friday is more loved by me than a voluntary pilgrimage to Meccah."

Saeed Bin Almusayeb
May Allah have mercy on him

7
The Importance of Friday Prayer

On a nice Friday afternoon, Khalifah Abdul Al-Malik Ibn Marwan entered the local mosque and began looking at the faces of the believers sitting in the prayer hall in search for his son Hisham, but couldn't find him. Then the call to prayer began and the Imam gave his Friday sermon. After the sermon was finished, the call to prayer was made again and all the believers stood up for prayer. After the prayer finished, the Khalifah began looking for his son again but sadly could not find him.

The Khalifah decided to send a messenger to his home to search for Hisham. When the messenger arrived, he knocked on the door and found Hisham at home.

The messenger asked him, "Hisham, why didn't you come to

Friday prayer today? Your father has been asking about you?"

Hisham answered, "Well... Our donkey was sick and not able to take me to the mosque and I couldn't find another animal to take me so I did not go today."

The messenger returned to the Khalifah to inform him what his son told him. The Khalifah was furious and asked the messenger to bring Hisham to the mosque so he could talk to him.

When Hisham arrived at the mosque, his father said, "Hisham, you did not come to the mosque today because you could not find an animal to bring you? Because of your actions, you may not use any animal for transportation for a whole year. You will have to walk to the mosque for the rest of this year!"

Source: Rawa'a al-Urayfi, page 49

Lessons Learned:

1. **Responsibility Towards our Children**
Even though the Khalifah had many other responsibilities, he did not forget his responsibility towards his son. He was implementing a saying from our Prophet Mohammed (PBUH) which says, *"Every one of you is a guardian and is responsible for his charge; the ruler is a guardian and is responsible for his subjects; the man is a guardian in his family and responsible for his charges; a woman is a guardian of her husband's house and responsible for her charges; and the servant is a guardian of his master's property and is responsible for his charge."* So, the responsibility does not only mean feeding, clothing, and educating our children. The true responsibility is to raise our children to have a spiritual connection with our faith and truly understand the religion. By truly understanding the faith, they will in return love the religion and follow it based on their own will, inshallah.

2. **Accountability and Following Up**
Many times we get angry at our children but always forget to hold them accountable for their mistake and follow up with them afterwards. This in return allows our children to repeat the same mistake and know they will get away with it. But as we noticed from this story that the Khalifah followed up in order to discover the reason for his son not coming to Friday prayer. He insisted on knowing the reason of his absence because Friday prayer is an obligation towards all male believers and its rewards are magnificent (Attending Friday prayer will eliminate all bad deeds from one Friday to the next).

3. **Excuses and Getting Away with Mistakes**
We rarely make excuses to miss opportunities for recreation or fun. But when a task involves a religious obligation, we often find a million excuses to steer away from doing

them (The animal was sick and not able to take me to the mosque). It is important to keep in mind that God watches everything and knows what lies hidden inside our hearts.
4. **Verbal Punishment is Stronger**
   The Khalifah did not send the punishment to his son Hisham with the messenger because it would not affect him as much. He brought him in front of him and verbally proclaimed his punishment to make him feel the significance of his mistake and the significance of disobeying Allah (SWT).
5. **The Importance of Friday Prayer**
   The Khalifah wanted to teach his son that Friday is one of the most important days and all must attend this prayer leaving behind all jobs and/or activities. Not having a means of transportation is not an excuse to not attend this significant prayer, as Allah (SWT) says in his holy Quran: *"O you who have believed, when [the adhan] is called for the prayer on the day of Jumu'ah [Friday], then proceed to the remembrance of Allah and leave trade. That is better for you, if you only knew."* [Al-Jumu'a:9].
6. **Severity of the Punishment**
   The punishment of walking to the mosque for a whole year was severe enough to teach him a good lesson. It's obvious that part of the reason Hisham missed the prayer was because the walking distance was very long and the weather outside was very hot, and therefore why he did not walk to the mosque. Thus, the Khalifah chose a wise punishment that would teach him a lesson so he would never repeat the same mistake again.

"The first thing that you will lose from your faith is humility, and the last thing you will lose is your prayer. Perhaps, there will be one who prays who has no good in him, who is about to enter a mosque and will not see amongst them a humble person."

Huthaifa Bin Alyamama
May Allah be pleased with him

— 8 —
Reverence in Prayer

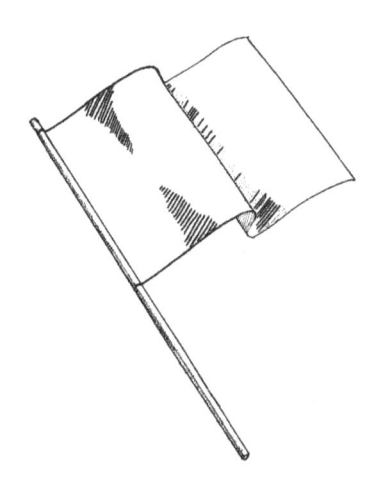

It was said that one day King Aurangzeb was leading the Muslims in a battle against Abdulaziz Al-Balkhi. At some point during the battle it was time for Zuhr prayer though the battle was at its peak. To everyone's surprise, the king got off his horse and lined up for prayer along with the soldiers who were with him. Fearing for his life, his friends pleaded with him to pray later. Instead, the king performed the prayer in the best way possible; he perfected his bows, prostration and reverence and was indifferent to what was happening around him. His enemies were so disheartened by what they saw that they requested a truce with the Muslims, saying, "Fighting these men is defeat itself."

Source: Tarikh al-Dawa al-Islami fil-Hind, p.122

Lessons Learned:

Prayer Should Always Be on Time
Devout Muslims are aware that prayer must be on time in compliance to the verse: *"Indeed, prayer has been decreed upon the believers a decree of specified times."* [An-Nisa:103]. Notice in the story that despite the extreme danger of the situation they listened to the call of prayer confident that Allah (SWT) will have mercy on them. Even during war, prayer times should be respected, but due to the difficult nature of war, the Prophet (PBUH) used to have the Muslim soldiers pray in two shifts.

1. **Allah's (SWT) Alliance**
The close friends and advisors of the king advised him not to pray at that time so the enemy would not have the opportunity to kill him. The king refused to listen to this advice and chose to stand between the hands of Allah (SWT) knowing that those who stand with Allah (SWT) are protected by Allah (SWT) always.
2. **Tranquility and Reverence is the Foundation for Prayer Acceptance**
Some would have rushed their prayer in this difficult situation filled with fear and anxiety or may have looked around vigilantly for danger and not performed their prayer correctly. This leader stood between the hands of Allah (SWT) knowing that He is the only one who could protect them. Allah (SWT) endowed tranquility and reassured his heart as he turned to Allah (SWT) for strength and protection.
3. **Victory is from Allah**
We notice that when the king chose to trust Allah (SWT) alone and performed the prayer, then Allah (SWT) granted him victory according to the verse: *"And whoever fears Allah - He will make for him a way out"* [At-Talaq:2]. Allah (SWT) instilled fear in the hearts of the enemy. The enemy's leader admitted that fighting these men was defeat

itself.
4. **Gaining Status**
   When you perform your prayer and religious duties, others will respect you and you will gain status and strength. This strength is extended from Allah's (SWT) strength. If Allah (SWT) was to abandon you, then you would be small and insignificant. You must respect your religion and your duties so that others will respect you even if those people disagree with your opinions or beliefs.

"The devil ties three knots on the back of a person's head while they are sleeping. If a person wakes up and remembers Allah the Almighty, one knot will be untied. If a person performs ablution, another knot is untied. If a person prays the last knot will be untied. The person wakes up energetic, not mean spirited and lazy."

Prophet Muhammed
Peace and blessings be upon him

— 9 —
The Importance of Fajr Prayer

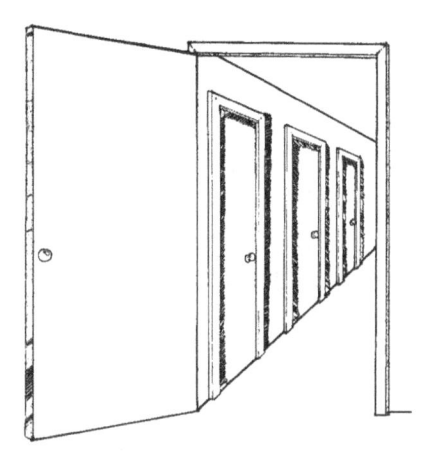

One day, Imam Ahmed Ibn Hanbal was walking and noticed a man robbing people as they passed by. The people ran trying to catch the thief and shouted, but the thief tried to hide to avoid being caught.

The next morning, Imam Ahmed Ibn Hanbal went to the mosque for Fajr prayer. As he entered the mosque, he noticed the thief from the previous day standing up to pray Fajr. He kindly went up to him and said, "My friend, the actions you did yesterday do not match what you are doing today. Our lord will not accept your prayer if you continue the actions you did yesterday." The thief answered, "Imam, between my God and I are many closed doors, so I thought I should at least keep one door open in hope that Allah (SWT) will open the remaining closed doors." Imam Ahmed Ibn Hanbal was surprised by his response and told him, "InshaAllah!"

A couple of months passed and Imam Ahmed Ibn Hanbal went to Mecca to perform the obligation of Hajj. As he was circling around the Ka`bah, he noticed a man hanging on to the Ka`bah and crying in plea to his Lord, "Lord, I sincerely repent all my wrong doings. If you don't accept my repentance then who will? Bestow upon me your mercy and forgiveness, for if you don't, then who will? Lord, I will never go back to doing bad again, please help me by forgiving me and giving me strength to stay away from bad!" Imam Ahmed Ibn Hanbal stopped and began to stare at the believer who was pleading to his Lord. Then he noticed that the pleading man was the same thief that had robbed his neighborhood!! Imam Ibn Hanbal told himself, "SubhanAllah, he left one door open with Allah (SWT) and Allah (SWT) opened all the other doors for him!"

Source: Dr. Saud ibn Ibrahim al-Shuraim, Muntada ahl-al-Sunnah wal-Jamma'ah among other sources

Lessons Learned:

1. **Advice and its Etiquette**
   We notice that Imam Ahmed Ibn Hanbal tried to advise the robber kindly without professing exactly what he did to avoid embarrassing him in the middle of the mosque. He simply told him that the actions you did yesterday do not match the actions you are doing now. Furthermore, the advice he made was based on the indication that doing wrong does not suit the actions of true believers.
2. **Prayer and Its Importance**
   We notice that the robber wanted to keep the most important relationship between the servant and his Lord, the prayer. He broke many rules and ignored all the other ties but kept the tie that will return him to his Lord. For prayer is the reason that all our good deeds are accepted and the reason for us to acknowledge our wrong doings and pray for Allah (SWT)'s forgiveness and mercy, it is in order to gain His forgiveness and enter paradise inshallah.
3. **Importance of Fajr Prayer and its Protection**
   The robber knew that persisting in praying Fajr prayer is the best option to stay close to Allah (SWT) because praying Fajr prayer with a group in the masjid equals staying up half the night worshipping God and by praying Fajr one will remain in Allah (SWT)'s protection all day long. As the Prophet (PBUH) said, *"Those who pray Fajr stay in Allah's protection."* Narrated by Muslim.
4. **Self Blame**
   From the robbers answer to Imam Ahmed we notice that he knows his mistakes and blames himself for the wrong-doings and is trying to overcome them. Those who do wrong and admit to it will always hold themselves accountable and pray for forgiveness and inshallah will be forgiven. But those who don't admit to their mistakes and don't want to change will find it very hard to repent.

5. **Believing and Encouraging**
   Even though Imam Ahmed was surprised by the robber's response he didn't laugh or mock him, but believed him and encouraged him by saying, "inshaallah!"
6. **The Hajj that is Accepted**
   We notice that the robber chose the best action to cleanse him from his sins and impurities, the hajj. The hajj that is accepted doesn't have any reward but Jennah. As the Prophet Muhammad (PBUH) says, *"One who performs Hajj in His way and doesn't speak obscene language, and doesn't commit sins, will come back [purified] as he was at the time of his birth."* (Bukhari: No. 1421)
7. **Persistence of the Acts of Worship**
   We notice that the robber did not say I am a robber so Allah (SWT) will not accept my prayers. But he stayed persistent on the acts of worship in the hope of being cured from the sickness or falling further into the ruins, god forbid. We often put people down who lie or make mistakes, yet if they come to seek forgiveness, we often make their problem worse by letting them lose any hope of forgiveness. Allah (SWT) is merciful and he knows what is inside our hearts.
8. **Allah (SWT) is Merciful**
   We notice that Allah (SWT) loves his believers, so if one of us gets closer by walking to Him, He will come running to us. So let us be generous to Allah (SWT) with worship and God will be generous in accepting and doubling our rewards. Allah (SWT) will make available to us more opportunities to earn good deeds and will present us with the greatest rewards in this life and the hereafter. Just as when the robber knocked on one door, Allah (SWT) answered him by opening all the doors to him.

"If there are three men in a village or desert and salah is not established among them, then the Satan takes mastery over them. So be with the congregation since the wolf devours the remote (Stray) sheep."

Prophet Muhammed
Peace and blessings be upon him

— 10 —
The Importance of Praying with a Group

There once was a man named Amer Ibn Al-Zubair. He was a very wise man and the one thing he hated most in life is to have his time wasted. He tried his best to always fill his time by doing things that please Allah (SWT). He also made sure that there was an Islamic book, or the Quran close to him to read. Everyday, he woke up for Fajr prayer and headed to the mosque. After he finished praying, he would pick up one of the Islamic books and immerse himself in the book. After he left the mosque, he made it a habit to visit the cemetery to pray for all the dead Muslims in their graves. Even though he may not have ever known any of the dead people there, he loved doing this because they were his brothers and sisters in Islam. Then, after spending some time there he would return back to his home.

When Amer Ibn Al-Zubair walked in the streets, his neighbors used to invite him to come and enjoy the evening with them. He used to always tell them, "I don't enjoy spending time eating my brother's dead flesh by backbiting about him or our other brothers in Islam. There is no better place to sit and spend time other than the cemetery because it reminds you of where you will be one day and no better books to spend your time reading than the Quran and Islamic books."

Every time Amer made sujud he made a special dua, "Dear God, I ask you for a good death." So his children asked him one day, "Dad, what is a good death?" He answered, "Kids, I pray to God that when my time comes to die, I want to die while I am making solemn sujud to him."

After a couple of years, Amer grew very old and ill. It was very hard for him to move and walk to the masjid and do all the wonderful habits he was accustomed to doing over the years. One day he heard the athan for Maghrib prayer. He told his children to please take him to the masjid so he can pray Maghrib there. His children told him, "Dad, you don't have to. You are sick and God gives people who are sick allowance to miss the prayer in the masjid." He told them, "You think I can actually hear 'Come to Pray, Come to great rewards' and not go?" So all his children gathered around him and carried him to the masjid on their shoulders. He prayed sitting down that day because he just could not stand up, and while making his last sajdah of the prayer he died.

Source: Al-Zuhd by Imam Ahmed ibn Hanbal, Aa'id al-Qarni

Lessons Learned:

1. **The Variety of Ways to do Good Deeds**
   We can learn from Amer the many different ways to be close to Allah (SWT). From Praying in the masjid, to reading Islamic books to increase our knowledge, to visiting the cemetery and praying for our lost brothers and sisters in Islam. How many of us can do these good deeds and remain consistent in doing them?
2. **Taking Advantage of Time**
   We notice from this story that Amir never left room in his day to waste time. He tried his best to take advantage of every moment in his life because he understood that we will be asked about it on the Day of Judgment. Because he knew that he would be spending the entire morning at the masjid and there is a long break from one prayer to another, therefore, he made sure to bring a book along to take advantage of the time in the masjid. After the masjid, he went to the graveyard to remind himself of the hereafter and how he should work hard in this life so he can enjoy the hereafter.
3. **Mistakes Made When Friends Get Together**
   We easily fall into this problem daily. We might have vowed never to backbite again but are placed in situations that force us to backbite. We notice that Amer in this story refused to get together with his neighbors because he didn't want to open the door to gain bad deeds.
4. **Visiting the Graveyard**
   We often pass by the graveyard without even looking at it or are afraid of going in at times. Amir, in this story, forced himself to visit the graveyard daily. He wanted to be reminded daily that this is where he will end up. Imagine if we were reminded daily of where we are all headed. Would we really continue to do things that disappoint Allah (SWT)? Would we ever miss prayers? Or backbite? We

need to always remind ourselves that we will all die someday and the opportunity to do good will end. We have to take advantage of every moment before we run out of time.

5. **The Perfect Death**

   We all wish to die while we are praying or doing something for the sake of Allah (SWT) but not many of us will have our wish come true. Why? As we noticed from Amir that he worked very hard for this wish to come true. He was persistent and dedicated his life to make his wish come true. How many of us really do that?

6. **Praying with a Group**

   It's very hard at times to take ourselves from our worldly tasks to pray, let alone going to the local mosque to conduct this prayer with a group. But if we only understood the reward, we would make it our goal like Amir to make it to the mosque and pray with a group. Our beloved Prophet's (PBUH) hadith dictates, *"Whoever prays forty days in congregation to Allah, catching the opening takbir of the Imam, Allah will grant two disclaimers: the disavowal of hell and the disavowal of hypocrisy."* (Reported by Tirmidhi and authenticated by Albany). Amer, in the story, to the last moment refused to miss the opportunity of praying in the house of God. Remember, he had a lifetime wish to die while making sujud and was persistent in making his wish come true. Therefore, he did not allow any worldly tasks or illness to make him forget his wish in life. There are such great opportunities for reward, May Allah (SWT) guide us to the right path.

7. **Supplication- The Brains of Worship**

   Alongside all the good activities Amer practiced daily for the sake of Allah (SWT), he never stopped making supplication (Dua). He knew that supplication is the fastest way one can reach Allah (SWT). Because he was persistent in his supplication and never gave up, Allah (SWT) rewarded him by taking his life at a moment where the believer is the closest to Allah (SWT), the sujud. We can only pray that

Allah (SWT) accepts us as his true believers and gives us good deaths InshAllah.

Tawus Ibn Kaysan may Allah have mercy on him used to jump out of his bed startled. Then purified and faced the Qibla until morning and said, "The thought of hellfire took away the sleep of the worshippers."

— 11 —
Midnight Prayers

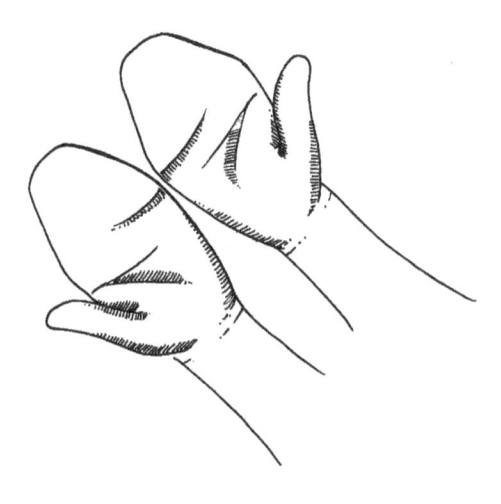

One day, I was roaming the bazaars of Baghdad when I came upon a young servant. She was being sold for only ten dinars. The price was so cheap and yet the owner claimed that there was nothing wrong with her.

"What a catch," I told myself, "she could certainly be a great help around the house." So, I bought her and took her home.

As soon as we arrived home, I offered the young woman food. I assumed that she might be hungry. She didn't touch the food, and in fact, she was a bit surprised. She said, "My lord, I have never seen anyone eat during this time of the day, ever!" I left her alone and went on with my business. Later that night, I offered her some food again and she ate a little.

After dinner, she asked, "My lord, can I be of help?" I said that I didn't need anything. She said, "If I may be excused, I shall fulfill my duties toward God, the greatest Master of all," and went to her room.

I prayed Isha and went straight to sleep. In the middle of the night I heard a knocking on my door. I was startled. "What is it?" I asked.

"It is I, my lord, your servant." She answered.

"What is the matter? Is something wrong?"

"Nothing is the matter, sir. I just want to bring to your attention that it is now the time for the midnight prayers."

"Is that it? Leave me alone!" I yelled.

A while later she comes knocking on my door again! "My lord, if you like, you still have some time to read a little bit of Qura'n."

What nerve she has, I thought to myself, to come knocking on my door twice in the middle of the night! "Listen carefully, young lady," I said, "during the day, I work like a dog, and during the night, I sleep like a log!"

She left, but only for a little while. This time, she came pounding on my door! "Don't you yearn for God's forgiveness and mercy? Don't you want to come closer to God and find peace and comfort? The time has come for YOU to wake up and take your place among the worshippers and express your servitude to your Lord!"

Her words were moving and touching, I couldn't help but rush to the washroom, perfect my ablution, and pray. When I finished, she, was still praying. She was whispering her supplications to God. I couldn't hear, so I came closer. She was saying, "Oh God, I know you love me, thus, you shall forgive me."

When she finished, I asked her "What makes you so sure that God loves you?"

She replied, "What could it be, then, if not love; that I am chosen to pray in the middle of the night, while YOU are left asleep?"

Indeed, it be must be love, I thought to myself. Praying the midnight prayers is a privilege that not many people achieve. "Go on young lady, for you are free from servitude for the sake of God."

She was grateful and humble. As she left, she made a supplication to God, "My Lord, this is the smaller freedom. Now, I await the true liberty; to be released from hellfire."

Source: Daqa'iq al-Layl al-Ghaliyah, Safaqaat Rabihah by Khalid Abu Shadi

Lessons Learned:

1. **You Can Buy Something Inexpensive, Yet it Can be Very Valuable**
   The servant was not expensive in terms of money, but she was extremely valuable in terms of knowledge and understanding the love of God. She taught her master a very important lesson about loving and serving God.
2. **Belief is Not Verbal, Rather it's Practical**
   The servant was fasting, but she did not mention it to her master when he offered her food. When the time came to eat, she ate just enough to maintain her health and acquire enough energy to perform her duties.
3. **One Who Leads Others to Acts of Goodness is Rewarded as if he Performed it Himself**
   It wasn't enough for the servant to pray her midnight prayers alone. She wanted her master to be rewarded as well. Since the servant was the one to advise him to pray, she will be receiving the reward for his prayers as well.
4. **Spreading the Word of God Takes Patience and Consistency**
   The servant tried to wake her master up three times. She didn't give up, nor did she lose her patience. She tried the first third of the night, then again at midnight and a third time towards the last third of the night, until he finally stood up to pray.
5. **It Takes Perseverance to Defeat the Evil Within Ourselves**
   After three trials, the man was finally able to beat his urge to stay asleep in his cozy bed. The man made the right decision to get up and pray. Our life is a constant battle between the right thing to do and what we desire; we can win it one choice at a time.
6. **Love of God**
   God truly loves you when you are blessed to do acts of

good. When we do acts of good, it's because we have the intention, and God helps us do it; we do not act upon it on our own; rather it is a blessing from God.

7. **The Importance of Midnight Prayer**
The servant appreciated the bounties of midnight prayers. The Prophet (PBUH) said: *"You should pray qiyaam al-layl, for it is the custom of the righteous who came before you and it brings you closer to your Lord, and expiates sins and prevents misdeeds"* Narrated by al-Tirmidhi, 3549.

8. **The Importance of Thinking Positively About God**
The servant believes it is the generosity of God that set her free from this master, and she is hopeful that she will be free from hellfire.

Some Scholars said: "The truth saves you even if you are afraid. And lying brings you down even if you feel it's safe."

— 12 —
Honesty is Your Protector

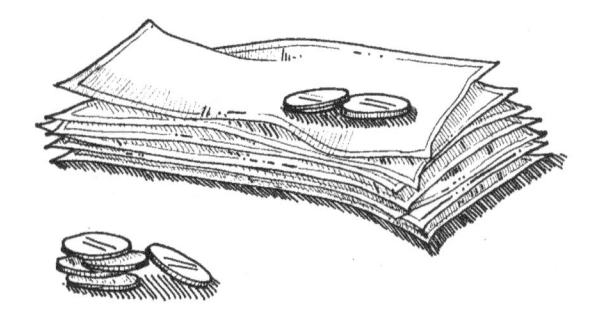

It was narrated that Sheikh Abdul Qadir Al-Jilani, once said, "I have lived by honesty my entire life." He continued, "When I was a young man, I travelled from Makkah to Baghdad seeking Islamic knowledge. My mother gave me forty Dinars (Gold coins) and made me promise to be honest."

When we reached the land of Hamdan, thieves attacked us and took everything we had in our caravan. One thief approached me saying, "What do you have in your belongings?" and I replied, "I have forty Dinars."

The thief thought that I was mocking him, so he let me be. Another thief came up to me and asked me the same question and I replied with the same answer, so he took me to their leader.

The leader asked me what I had in my belongings and I told him. The leader then asked me, "What is it that is making you tell the truth?" So I told him that my mother had made me promise to always tell the truth, and I would never break a promise with her.

After listening to this, the leader began to cry and said, "You are worried about breaking a promise with your mother, and I do not fear breaking a promise with Allah!!" The leader then ordered his men to return all the looted things to the caravan and said, "I ask Allah for His forgiveness because of what I've learnt from this young man."

The men who were with him said, "You were our leader when we were thieves, and now you are our leader in repenting," then they all asked Allah (SWT) for His forgiveness because of the young man's honesty.

Source: Salah al-Ummah fi 'Uluw al-Himmah, p.45, by Syed Hussain al-Affani

Lessons Learned:

1. **The Importance of Knowledge**
   The mother gave her son everything she owned for him to seek knowledge, as she knew that if her son gained knowledge, he would learn everything he needed to do well in this life and she and her son would receive rewards in this life. They would also receive the reward of all the students he would teach without those students losing any of their own reward.
2. **Mothers are Teachers**
   The mother wanted to teach her son an important lesson, for him to build his life upon both in this life and the afterlife, and that lesson was honesty. She knew honesty would keep him well in this life and would diminish his bad deeds in the afterlife, as mentioned in the verse: *"O you who have believed, fear Allah and speak words of appropriate justice. He will [then] amend for you your deeds and forgive you your sins. And whoever obeys Allah and His Messenger has certainly attained a great attainment."* [Al-Ahzab:70-71]
3. **Honesty and Keeping Promises**
   Abdul Qadir was honest with his enemies despite knowing that doing so would make him lose all his money, but he chose to keep his promise to his mom and his promise to Allah. Anyone who keeps his promise to Allah (SWT) will definitely be with Him.
4. **What People Say and its Effect on an Individual**
   Many people lie or change what they say, fearing the person(s) in front of them, or avoiding ridicule, or wanting to gain approval and admiration from others. Abdul Qadir heard the thief mocking him and did not care and persisted in being honest. He understood that Allah's approval of him was more important than other people's opinion; those who seek Allah's affection and approval will also gain it from others.

5. **Honesty Could Save You**
   Abdul Qadir's honesty was rewarded by Allah saving his money, and granting him good deeds for the thieves' repentance. One can never know when something so simple as keeping a promise might open many doors of happiness and opportunities.
6. **The Blessings and Good that Accompany Honesty**
   As a result of Abdul Qadir's honesty, Allah sent his blessings to the whole caravan by having everyone's belongings returned to them. Honesty brings forth Allah's blessings.
7. **One Small Incident Can Guide an Entire Group**
   The leader was moved when he saw the young man insisting on telling the truth and keeping his promise. The whole group repented when they saw their leader doing so.
8. **The Righteousness of a Leader Leads to the Righteousness of the Followers**
   If you are a leader among your friends, and you do good actions, your friends or followers will follow you in doing the same. You will gain the good deeds of your friends, without them losing any of their good deeds. The same happened with the thieves' leader; when he asked for Allah's forgiveness and repented, his followers did the same. Always be the light of righteousness for your followers.

"And the one who has brought the truth and [they who] believed in it - those are the righteous."

[Az-Zumar:33]

—— 13 ——
Being Truthful With the Prophet (PBUH)

It was one hot summer afternoon, too hot to play outside. I went inside and played all the indoor activities. Soon enough, I got bored so I decided to go sit with my grandpa. He always had a nice story to tell me. "Grandpa, can you tell me one of your stories?" I asked him nicely. "Sure, just come have a seat next to me and I will tell you a story about our beloved Prophet Muhammad (PBUH)."

In the summer of the ninth year of Hijrah, the Romans gathered forty thousand soldiers to fight Prophet Mohammed (PBUH) and his army. When the Prophet (PBUH) heard of this news, he quickly called for all the Muslim men to leave everything and join him in battle. Thirty thousand troops gathered by the side of the Prophet (PBUH) ready to fight the Roman soldiers.

In the stifling heat the soldiers barged down the road ready for war. This war was named the war of Tabook. Once the Muslim army reached the war ground, the enemy began to negotiate and reached an agreement with the Muslims to cease fire and not have war. All the Muslims were very happy and went back to their homes.

As they were going back, the Prophet Mohammed (PBUH) noticed that there were some men missing who had not joined them in the war. Upon his return, Prophet Mohammed (PBUH) called upon those who had not joined them. Many of them lied to the Prophet (PBUH) and told him excuses. Three men could not dare tell a lie to our beloved Prophet Mohammed (PBUH) and they were Ka`ab Ibn Malek, Mararah Ibn Rabee`, and Hilal Ibn Umayah. Ka'ab Ibn Malek told Prophet Mohammed (PBUH), "We can't lie to you, oh Prophet Mohammed (PBUH), because sooner or later you will find out from Allah (SWT). I had the strength, and enough money to leave behind with my family to survive on and I had no excuse not to come to fight with you, oh Prophet (PBUH). I am extremely sorry and regret my actions. Please forgive me." Prophet Mohammed (PBUH) answered him, "Go back to your homes as I don't know how to deal with you. We will have to wait until I get a revelation about how to handle you."

The entire town was told not talk to the three men at all. Mararah and Hilal stayed home crying about the wrong decisions they made. Ka`ab went to town and tried to keep his life as normal as possible but nobody talked to him at all in town. After thirty days, the Prophet (PBUH) ordered the wives of these men to ignore them as well. Ka'ab was beginning to lose his patience and the hope of Allah (SWT)'s forgiveness.

A couple of days later a man came from the Roman Empire to Ka'ab. He came with a letter from the king of Ghassan and informed Ka'ab, "Since your people do not respect you and do not want you anymore, come join us in our city and we will gladly take you in." Ka`ab stared at him with fire torching from his eyes. He took the letter the man came with and ripped it into pieces then burned it.

He reminded himself that these are tricks from shaytan and he needed to be more patient. He believed in God and was not going to let anything shake his belief even though the whole world had turned against him. He increased his prayers, made much dua, and gave a lot of donations to the poor.

After forty days, on a Thursday morning, a revelation came to forgive the three men. Ka`ab's friends ran to his house to inform him about the good news. They were all grateful that Allah (SWT) and his Prophet (PBUH) had forgiven him. Ka`ab ran to the Prophet (PBUH) and thanked him for forgiving him. The Prophet (PBUH) said, "Don't thank me; thank Allah (SWT) that forgave you!" Ka`ab agreed and thanked Allah (SWT) and said, "I have given all my money and wealth for the sake of Allah (SWT) to the poor." The Prophet (PBUH) said, "Why did you give it all? You should have kept a little to live off of." Ka`ab answered, "Dear Prophet (PBUH), nothing rescued me and gave me honor but telling the truth. I vow never to tell a lie again."

Source: Al-Sirah al-Nabawiyyah, p.298-p.300, by Muhammad Said Ramadan al-Bouti

Lessons Learned:

1. **Tough Times Reveal One in Truth**
   We all get lazy at times, lazy enough to miss a couple of prayers because of a TV show and lazy enough not to fast in the summer time. Ka`ab in this story was lazy. He did not want to go fight the war in the summer, it was just too hot! He did not think of the great rewards in the hereafter or what will happen when he did not respond to a request from our dear Prophet (PBUH). How many of us fall into this same scenario? Only those who have strong faith and hope will be able to stand strong in tough times. We can only pray that God increase our faith and hope in him to be able to overcome all the tough times in our lives.

   Lying to the Prophet (PBUH)
   those who lied to the Prophet (PBUH) didn't understand the massive punishment attached to it. There is a Hadith that says:
   "Falsely attributing something to me is not like falsely attributing something to anyone else. Let the one who knowingly lies about me take a seat in Hellfire." Prophet Muhammad (PBUH) (Related by Muslim)
   Lying itself is wrong but lying to our beloved Prophet (PBUH) is a major sin. If left without repentance it can lead one to enter the hell fire. How often do we tell lies? Or lie to ourselves? May God forgive us for telling the lies we did and help us remove this bad habit from our personalities.

   Being Truthful with the Prophet (PBUH)
   SubhanAllah, Ka`ab could not get himself to tell a lie because he was ashamed of himself in front of the Prophet (PBUH). He knew if he lied, the Prophet (PBUH) would find out. How many of us think before we lie? We are often quick to tell a lie immediately and forget that Allah (SWT) never sleeps and is always watching us. Are we not ashamed of ourselves that Allah (SWT) knows that we lie?

2. **The Importance of Jihad**
   In this war Allah (SWT) wanted to teach his believers that no matter what the circumstances are when there is a call to war one should leave everything and obey the call. As Allah (SWT) says *"Go forth, whether light or heavy, and strive with your wealth and your lives in the cause of Allah. That is better for you, if you only knew."* [At-Tawba:41]. So we noticed the great punishment of ignoring them that Allah (SWT) bestowed upon the men who did not obey his orders.
3. **Listening and Obeying**
   The three men were part of the society. They had friends, relatives, neighbors who talked to them and enjoyed their company. But when Prophet (PBUH) ordered the town to stop talking to them, they all obeyed without thinking twice about it, to the point that they didn't even return the salaam which is an obligation.
4. **Obeying Allah (SWT) and His Prophet Over Obeying your Spouse**
   Islam highlights the importance of women obeying their husbands. There is a saying for the Prophet (PBUH) that says, *"If a woman prays her five obligatory prayers, fasts her month, guards her chastity, and listens to her husband, it will be said to her: Enter paradise from any door you desire."* (Narrated by Imam Ahmad). But obeying Allah and his messenger is even more powerful. We notice in the story that the punishment reached a point that the Prophet ordered the men's wives to not talk to them as well and ignore them. This is momentous; imagine your wife not talking to you for a mistake you did with Allah (SWT). The wives were not afraid nor felt sorry for their husbands. They did as they were told. Also, the men did not fight with their women. They understood the punishment and accepted it as is. How many of us can be patient and accept punishment our parents put upon us?
5. **The Wolf Cannot Eat A Strong Sheep**

We notice in the story that when Ka`ab was at his weakest, the enemies came to get him to join their religion. The shaytan knows very well when to strike. He strikes when the believer is at his weakest point and opens opportunities for him to easily fall into the wrong path. Ka`ab, Alhamdulillah, was smart and didn't fall into the Satan's trap again. He stayed strong and understood that this was a test from God. So instead of accepting the enemy's offer, he went and prayed and asked for forgiveness from Allah (SWT). Also, he did not allow his enemy to notice his weakness and problem. How many of us are strong enough to say "no" to the many worldly pleasures out there that move us away from Allah (SWT)?

6. **Returning to Allah (SWT) When We Have Problems**
We notice in the story that when the three men felt their mistake, they went directly to Allah (SWT) to ask for forgiveness. They tried three different ways to gain forgiveness:
   a. **Dua**: They continued to make duaa and ask for repentance repeatedly.
   b. **Prayer**: They increased their prayers and cried in it out of sincerity.
   c. **Acceptance**: They accepted the punishment as is and didn't object to Allah's (SWT) plans for them.

7. **Relief and Being Thankful**
When Ka`ab heard that he had been forgiven he ran to the Prophet (PBUH) to thank him for forgiving him. Then the Prophet (PBUH) reminded him that he shouldn't thank him, he should thank Allah (SWT) for forgiving him. Ka`ab then immediately made sujud thanking Allah (SWT) for his forgiveness and gave zakat. We should thank Allah (SWT) for his uncountable blessings by praying, making dua, and giving zakat. We should thank Allah (SWT) by actions not by words only.

"The one who attains the most is not the one who prays a lot or fast many days. The one who truly attains most is from the generosity of the soul, a heart free from unjustified hate and the sincere conduct to the Muslim nation."

Alfadeel bin Alayad

14
Price of Honesty

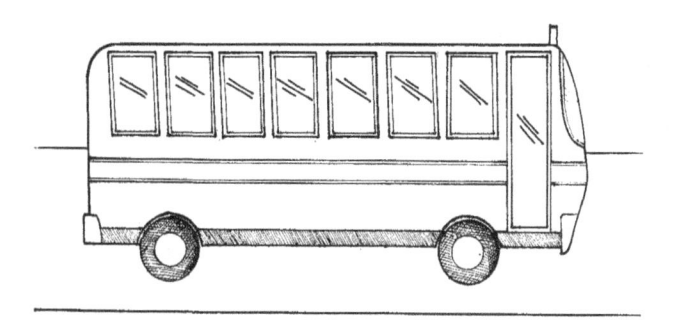

Several years ago an Imam moved to London. He often took the bus from his home to the downtown area. Some weeks after he arrived, he had occasion to ride the same bus. When he sat down, he discovered that the driver had accidentally given him twenty pence too much change. As he considered what to do, he thought to himself, 'you better give the twenty pence back. It would be wrong to keep it'.

Then he thought, 'oh forget it, it's only twenty pence. Who would worry about such a little amount? The bus company already takes so much fare, they will never miss it anyway. Accept it as a gift from God Almighty and keep quiet'.

When his stop came, the Imam paused momentarily at the door.

He handed the twenty pence back to the driver and said, "Here, you gave me too much change."

The driver replied with a smile, "Aren't you the new Imam in this area? I have been thinking lately about going to worship at your mosque. I just wanted to see what you would do if I gave you too much change!"

When the Imam stepped off the bus, his knees became weak and soft. He had to grab the nearest light pole and hold for support, the imam looked up to the heavens and cried:

"Oh God, I almost sold Islam for twenty pence!"

Source: Majallat At-Tarbiyyah Al-Islamiyyah, 9th Edition, page 47

Lessons Learned:

1. **Morals Reflect our Beliefs**
   The driver wanted to know what Islam is about, so he tested the Imam. The driver thought however the Imam acts, it must be coming from his values and belief.
2. **Be an Ambassador for Islam**
   As Muslims who live in a non-Muslim country, we are representatives of our religion and culture. Islam will be judged through our clothing and actions. Be careful and be honest every day, because you never know who is watching!
3. **Be Aware of Satan's Temptations**
   Although the Imam was a strong believer, he almost fell into the trap of Satan. Satan suggested that the little change was not really worth returning, and to consider it a gift from God! We all know that gifts are usually given willfully and not by mistake. Satan is always around you trying to lead you astray, so be careful and subtle.
4. **Hold on to the True Teachings of Islam Wherever One May Be**
   The bus driver respected the Imam's integrity, and indicated his interest in Islam. The driver's first impression about Islam was positive after this experience, and was happy to meet such an honest man.
5. **Good Acts Prevent the Trap of Satan's Temptation**
   With certainty we can tell that the Imam has done many good deeds through his life. Merciful God saved him from committing a sin because of his piety.
6. **Actions Speak Louder Than Words**
   Many people preach about Islam, and how it is the religion of peace, forgiveness, and good. Yet, their own actions prove the opposite of what they say. We may never see the impact our actions have on people. Sometimes we may be the only representation of Islam a non-Muslim will see. Let

us be an example for others to see.
7. **Be Humble and Thankful to God**
   Many of us believe that when we do good, it's because we are good people. The truth is our soul is prone to evil, and due to our weakness, we are easily led by temptation, unless the Lord does bestow His Mercy and guide us toward righteousness.

"The leaf of a berry has one taste. However, if eaten by a silkworm the result will be silk. If eaten by a bee the result will be honey. If eaten by a baby deer the result will be a sweet smell. If eaten by a goat, the result will be pure milk. Who made this one plant leaf bring about many results? Allah, the Almighty without a doubt, the creator of the amazing universe."

Imam Al'shafii

15
Abu Hanifa and the Atheist

The royal palace in Baghdad stood on the banks of the Tigris River during the Abbasid Empire. On a quiet afternoon the Caliph was meeting with his subjects. An atheist approached the assembly and said "I don't believe in God; there cannot be a God. This world and everything within came into being by itself. Everything within the universe is taking its course naturally. There is no being, nor creator. Bring me your best debater and I will debate this issue with him."

The caliph was quiet for a bit. He thought, "If I kill this man, people will say it's because what he said is true and I could not prove him wrong." So, he decided to send his messenger to call upon Imam Abu Hanifa Nu'man. Abu Hanifa was the greatest scholar and the best debater at the time.

The messenger went over the Tigris River to the other side of the city to tell Abu Hanifa that the Caliph wanted him to debate an atheist. Abu Hanifa said he would be on his way as soon as he completed an important matter.

Unfortunately, Abu Hanifa took some time. Actually, a very long time, hours went by, and the Caliph, the Muslims, and the atheist were waiting patiently for Abu Hanefa to arrive. The atheist said, "Your best debater is too scared! He knows he's wrong, and he can't prove that there is a God! I guarantee he will not turn up today."

It was sunset when Abu Hanifa showed up apologizing for the delay.

He explained what had happened to make him too late. "On my way here, you know I had to cross the river, but there was no boat. So, I had to wait for one to show. I waited for a few hours, and suddenly something amazing happened. I saw tree branches flying over the river and turning into even planks all by themselves. Then, nails appeared from nowhere and arranged themselves perfectly into the wood! It was unbelievable... After that, a hammer emerged from the bottom of the river and suddenly started to hit the nails on the wood planks. Can you believe it? Right in front of my eyes, a boat was made all by itself! I was astounded and shocked. It was a real boat, and it appeared to be constructed very well. I rode the boat, and here I am!"

The atheist burst out laughing very loudly and said, "O Abu Hanifa, I heard that you were the best debater of your time, and I heard that you were the wisest, the most knowledgeable amongst your people. But from seeing you today, I can say that you show none of these qualities. You speak of a boat appearing from nowhere, without someone having built it. Wood planks arranging themselves, nails positioning themselves, a hammer constructing the boat all by itself! You're talking ridiculous; I do not believe a word you say!"

Abu Hanifa smiled and said, "If you cannot believe that a boat came into being without a boat maker, when this is only a boat, how can you believe that the whole world, the universe, the stars, the oceans, and the planets came into being without a creator? What is this boat in comparison to the stars? What is this boat in comparison to the moon? What is this boat in comparison to yourself?"

The atheist was shocked and speechless.

He finally said, "I submit. You have told the truth, for this universe could not exist if it wasn't created by a creator, and with certainty that creator must be God!"

Source: Abu Hanifa maa al-Mulhid from Hayat al-Imam Abu Hanifa, lecture by Tareq Al-Suwaidan, among other sources including Ibn Kathir, Ibn Hazm, Ibn Taymiyyah, and the book Siyar Ahwal al-Nubala'

Lessons Learned:

1. **All Atheists Are the Same**
   Throughout the ages, atheists deny the existence of God, and try by all means to make up philosophical and logical evidence to refute God's existence. We still find them every day, everywhere; in school, college, in our place of work and in the media, so be aware and be prepared.
2. **Don't Be Arrogant**
   The arrogant are at a loss in this life and in the hereafter. Whatever blessing you experience; be it knowledge, money, talent, strength...etc, it is from God. All thanks and gratitude is due to God for He has given you all of these.
3. **The Wisdom of the Caliph**
   It is easier to silence people and restrict their opinion, than to convince them with our point of view. If you don't have the information or lack the skill of persuasion, admit to it and find someone who does. This is what the Caliph did when he sought Imam Abu Hanifa, who was the most knowledgeable and best debater at the time.
4. **Physical and Practical Proofs are the Strongest**
   Imam Abu Hanifa could have argued endlessly and possibly uselessly with the atheist without convincing him. Imam Abu Hanifa used a practical example to reach the young man's heart.
5. **Don't Be Hasty in Judging People**
   The atheist was hasty to judge Imam Abu Hanifa as being wrong and scared and as to be trying to avoid the debate. However, the atheist was shocked when he found Imam Abu Hanifa proving his convictions in such a compelling way. Therefore, don't rush in making conclusions. You never know; perhaps what seems useless can actually be beneficial for you.
6. **Be Respectful and Avoid Sarcasm**
   When Imam Abu Hanifa was telling his story, the atheist

mocked the Imam and ridiculed him. However, Imam Abu Hanifa didn't respond disrespectfully, rather he was polite and replied courteously, which was a major factor in persuading the young man to come around.

7. **God, the Creator, the Sustainer**
   Everything you see around you signifies God's power and majesty. Meditation and reflection upon God's creation is a kind of worship that brings you closer to your Sustainer. It constitutes the road to real knowledge of the Creator.